SEASONAL SHIFTS

The Journey From Our Breakdowns to Our Breakthroughs

Amas Israel
The StoryBook Poet

Jai Publishing House Incorporated
1230 Peachtree Street NE, 19th Floor
Atlanta, Georgia 30309
www.jaipublishing.com

The views expressed in this publication are those of the author and do not necessarily reflect the official policy or position of any other agency, organization, employer or company associated with the publisher.

Scripture quotations taken from the Holy Bible, King James Version. All rights reserved.

Printed in the United States of America

ISBN-13: 978-1-7366613-1-4

DISCLAIMER

The information provided within Seasonal Shifts is meant to assist with your daily life and it is not meant to force or make any demands to how you should or should not live. The author of Seasonal Shifts is not responsible for the results of any actions following the reading of this book.

My purpose in life is: To teach our people who they are and what they represent. I accept that I have to take one of the many steps by writing this book! I am your friend and resource. I am The StoryBook Poet.

— — — — – ✍

This book is written with the inspiration from my Father, Mother, Siblings, my Beloved Daughter, and every person who has believed they are somebody more than they are today.

TABLE OF CONTENTS

SEASONAL SHIFTS

The Journey From Our Breakdowns to Our
Breakthroughs

Amas Israel
The StoryBook Poet

Introduction

Can we all agree that a priority within each individual's life is balance?

As humans, we will strive, replace and do whatever is necessary to complete the priority of having balance. The areas we want to prioritize are family, work, friendships, community activities, etc., and when we do not accomplish that balance, it displays as a stronghold or what can be coined as an uphill battle.

The Bible tells us in James 1:8 (KJV), "A double minded man is unstable in all his ways."

This applies to us when we stop and think past religion or our feelings.

Two specific sections within our lives need to be exposed. With exposure comes an outcome that will reveal an understanding.

The Breakdown to The Breakthrough is a process that will vary throughout our seasons in life. You will be able to capitalize in both areas reading this book.

When we analyze where we are in our own lives, we should conclude that a process took place, and we did not randomly end up in our current state.

A process happened. We are not born criminals; we are not born to hate, we are not born to kill, steal or rob anyone.

What happened was a process that lead those individuals to those outcomes, and that is the same with our Breakdown to our Breakthrough.

At the end of this book, your life will be transformed, and you will have come out better than when you started reading. I trust you will enjoy and appreciate the easy flow.

————✍

As the reader, you will learn:

- What Is the Breakdown
- What Is the Breakthrough
- The Process of the Breakdown and the Breakthrough
- What Feelings and Emotions Are Associated With Each
- Practical Personal Management and Developmental Skills

Let's get started!

CHAPTER 1

The Breakdown

One of my favorite quotes that came into my life during my middle teenage years is, "Seek first to understand then to be understood."

That applies to us all in every way possible because if we do not understand what is taking place around us, how can we grow and become better individuals at home, at our workplaces, and in our communities?

For my life, it is evident to me that I have had many shares of breaking down. I had breakdowns involving family, friends, school situations, the football field, and sometimes even my workplace.

I sometimes felt I was going from 0 to 60 when the breakdown happened. It came like rushing water and sometimes felt like a drowning scenario.

That is surprisingly only half of what the breakdown is all about, and the spectacular part of what we will talk about is the process involved with the breakdown.

– – – – – ✍

My experiences with the breakdown have grown over time, yet it remains. As a child, my breakdowns came more from my interactions with my parents after I was given directions that I did not want to accept or corrected in school for bad behaviors.

As I grew, my breakdowns came through sports; school was part of it, just not behaviorally, but academically and sometimes within my community interactions.

I struggled with wanting to understand school and applying myself, which led to my breakdown.

— — — — – ✍

The definition attributed to the Breakdown is "to fail in strength or vitality." What does it mean when we fail in strength?

It means to become weakened within our physical body, spiritually, and/or mental capacity from an outside source.

We become weakened by that external source, and the emotions of hurt, fear, loss, and shame are introduced within us.

Hurt explains a physical, mental, and/or spiritual hurt. Fear explains a scared, intimidated, and/or the unknown component.

Loss explains the helplessness, confused, distracted emotional context, and shame explains an embarrassed, shocked, omitting behavioral pattern.

I have fought against these emotions in my life because of a false sense of what a man is supposed to be.

I brushed aside the signals that should have been catered to because of my ignorance of the mental understanding of what the breakdown entailed.

From this point, we will enter into the process of The Breakdown.

– – – – – ✍

The Process

We need to believe and accept that our lives are created with a process of events that happen over time.

There is not a random act that placed us into our circumstances. For us to make the right choices, we need the right information and understanding.

If we make the process of childbirth until adulthood, we can visually and personally see the process. When we have to use the bathroom, that is not a random act that comes out of nowhere.

The process occurs from the external source that then reveals itself through our mind, then we act with an emotional and/ or physical response.

The Breakdown happens with:

- The outside source: a person(s), a situation we are emotionally connected to, a physical, spiritual or emotional hurt.

- The internal: the mind is powerful and easily manipulated; the uncontrollable thoughts, the hurt, fear, loss, and shame start to uncover themselves. Negative thoughts are recurring and starting to establish themselves.

- Reveals back into the outside and is acted out: a verbal signal (crying, yelling, or screaming) and/or physical (fight, flight, or freeze).

- We all heard the term: "Dead-man walking." I've found this truth in my own life and for others; many of us aren't living out our purpose, and we are losing in our respective careers.

— — — — – ✍

This is not intended to place judgment on any selected person or group; however, if you feel convicted by this message, you have to choose change.

I intend to plant a seed that will grow and sprout into understanding. The life we live today affects our tomorrow.

— — — — – ✍

We need to understand the feelings associated with the Breakdown, which are: Hurt, Fear, Loss, and Shame.

As human beings, we will experience one, if not all the feelings, and we will remain in that cycle until we understand our exit.

I have always said the mind is powerful yet, easily manipulated if we are not careful with our surroundings and the information we choose to pay attention to.

We know it is hard to avoid some information within our homes, schools, at work, or on the television (with television being the easiest to control because we can turn it on and off).

Remember, we are talking about The Breakdown.

$$----✍$$

The soul deals with our emotions and those emotions of hurt, fear, loss, and shame.

The Breakdown is usually the calm before the storm. If we stop and look at the actions of individual humans and/or groups of people, we will notice the progress of their behaviors.

For example, The Breakdown may come from a negative attitude towards a person or persons, a person distancing themselves from something or someone, the silent treatment; it will never become physical initially.

Those are signs of The Breakdown or "the calm before the storm." We must be sensitive to those hints to deal with them properly.

If we choose not to take those signs seriously, then what happens is a burst of emotions explained through physical behaviors, and three examples are fight, flight, or freeze.

Why does this have to lead to a physical fight? Well, have you ever tried to interact with a dog while it is on heat?

Now I am not saying humans and dogs are the same; however, the example is the most important aspect.

Most of the time, we hear the term "0 to 60" to explain a person's erratic behaviors.

One thing we do not want to do is add fuel to the fire!

— — — — – 🖎

Fight, Flight, Freeze

One component of my life I have always discouraged is being vulnerable to situations and/or being vulnerable in front of people.

I haven't gotten over this reality for myself, and I know it is a common reality for many people.

During my early childhood days, I experienced each of the three: fight, flight, and freeze. I mainly found my place in the freeze category. I didn't realize why, but I later concluded that I do not like the person to person conflict.

Let us look around, and we can see these traits within our families, coworkers, and neighbors. You will gain an understanding of the fight, flight, and freeze aspects of The Breakdown.

— — — — – ✍

Fight

....

When you're in an uncomfortable position, why would a person consider the fight method?

Is that person working out of fear of the unknown? Does that person believe they have no other way?

Each question is important to be taken into consideration. However, let's work our way to peel back the fight method.

Looking at human behavior, we can develop common objectives for the fight: (some examples are)

- ◈ Insecurities
- ◈ Fear of the unknown
- ◈ Personal regret
- ◈ False sense of self‑worth
- ◈ Low self‑esteem
- ◈ Haven't applied or learned other prosocial methods
- ◈ Emotionally unstable
- ◈ Family upbringing

What are ways to overcome the fight method? I've worked within the space for over 5 years, directly impacting the lives of hundreds of youth and families who used this method as a response. Each bulletin collectively added to the youth or family's reasoning.

What it comes down to is everybody wants to be heard and understood. Speaking for myself, being misunderstood leaves a sour feeling, and it pushes a person away from wanting to interact properly.

— — — — — ✍

The suggestions when working or being directly impacted with the fight method is:

Reestablish self-worth

Reconnect with specific passions or hobbies to build on your purpose

Stop and Think and don't react to unstable emotions (hurt, fear, loss, and shame) by giving yourself a cool-down period, which is timed. The timed aspect will assist you with making sure you have the choice to make a proper decision

Spend time with yourself to nurture your mind (turn the tv off and technological devices) and write down your thoughts and ideas (journal).

Deep Breathing: Inhale for 4 seconds, hold for 7 seconds and exhale for 8 seconds. (No set amount of time, just until you are in your correct headset)

What you notice is the word (Rei), which means once more or again. I say (Re) because there was a point in your life where this area was not so transparent. Get back to the basics. Return to the point in your life where you remember all the dreams you wanted to pursue, the people you have that care about you even if it is just one. Get away from the "stuff" and find out about yourself.

Flight

The next method of choice when operating in The Breakdown is flight.

The flight aspect involves avoidance, runaway, and/or omitting. With this method comes unfinished agendas and the recurring past issues within our lives.

Forgiving is difficult for me, but I have grown to understand forgiveness better because it allows me to break loose of the potential stronghold on my life.

The flight method carries the extra weight that becomes too much for our life's work.

We have too many gifts and talents to remain wrapped up with an unforgiving heart. Some traits of the flight method are:

- Double-minded
- Lack of Self-worth
- Peer Pressure
- Has trouble with forgiveness
- Holds grudges
- Lack of consistency within life
- Easily influenced by social surrounds
- Loss sense of purpose and feeling from to family, friends, and/or community
- Suicidal thoughts/actions- The attempt to escape from a situation or person(s)

A portion of our life is unexplained and covered up because of our choice to leave it where it lies.

I remember from my childhood, I have left many issues unresolved, and they are mainly with family members. The interesting part is more than half of my unresolved issues have dealt with family who may not have known I had the issue with them.

That is much of our story; we assume the other person knows or should when in fact, we should address the situation in love.

Have you ever been to a family gathering, and the relative you have the unresolved issue with shows up? How do you feel about that? What type of emotions is going through your mind?

When you're in this flight mode, we see the actions of leaving out the room when one walks in, making facial gestures, being quiet when that relative comes around.

Why is that?

There could be so many reasons, but I want to focus on the constant voice within our mind telling us to remember what hurt he/she has done.

The process begins with identifying what has us avoiding because, as I like to mention, we need to overcome our obstacles.

While we may be holding the hurt feelings, the person who hurt us lives their lives, so why shouldn't you.

STOP running away and face the action with a process.

STOP and THINK about why you are upset and/or hurt (a series of words, actions, lying, stealing?).

Write them down so you can see the visual.

– – – – – ✍

The Bible tells us don't go to bed angry (Ephesians 4:26 KJV). That means you have 24 hours to resolve the conflict. I know that is a challenge for many of us; however, make it your duty to free yourself.

- \ -

Find out what you want your outcome to be. Set a timetable of how and when you will address the issue; the person may have already passed, so you have to work within yourself to tell yourself to forgive.

Write the word 'forgive' and hang it up on your bathroom mirror, post it on your car steering wheel, on your front door.

- \ -

Possibly look for assistance in someone you trust, speak to a close personal friend, be careful within this step because it is not about telling to gossip, but telling to closure.

- \ -

Address the person, and if the person doesn't want to talk with you, then give it time and try again. Do not chase them, but free yourself.

You do not always need an apology to free yourself; it comes down to having your mind made up to forgive to set you free, not to set them free.

There are so many great accomplishments you need to complete to remain stuck in neutral.

Freeze

We all have been stuck and looking for a quick answer that never seems to come or even a way out.

We have been stuck to the point where we have given up and/or didn't expect the situation to have that type of outcome. I have experienced this area in my life over the past few years because I didn't want to accept certain situations, and I wasn't ready to accept the crux of the matter.

We look around, and we see so many people freeze up, and what it shows us is:

- Confusion
- Double-mindedness
- Indecisiveness
- Shame
- Guilt
- Fearfulness

When we freeze, like when we fight incorrectly and/or flight, we misstep and avoid the opportunity to build something great.

Our opportunities that come through our Breakdown become null and void when we do not grasp what we have to get to where we need to be.

That is what the purpose of this book is for, to assist you to get to where you need to be and overcome where you are.

We do not need to have the victim mentality or have the false sense of thinking that the world owes us something. It does not mean there is no reality to your circumstance, but it means you do not have to stay in that situation.

Instead, if we start with the firm understanding that the world owes us nothing, we will start to condition our minds to go after everything we need.

I said, <u>need</u> not <u>want</u>, because sometimes what we want is not what we need at that specific time.

I admit life is a constant challenge, and we have to endure many challenges, and so many individuals have come through what they called "hell."

I do not downplay that; however, we all need to know the process of what we are going through because we no longer have to act out of order or misstep.

Our lives are too important to waste time and act as though we have all the time to keep misstepping.

— — — — — ✍

With that being said, some action steps to work within the freeze process are:

- Stop and Think about why you froze up– The Who, The What, and The Why. Get real and not make any explanation at this point.

- Identify 3 ways to address the situation –possibly need to involve a close friend/family member.

- Identify what would you like your outcome to be. Be very realistic and specific.

- Look for an opportunity to address the situation; if not possible, remember to address the situation within 24 hours.

The but

Every day we look around on social media, in our workplaces, our homes, and overall communities, we see so many people making negative excuses.

Those negative excuses come like rushing water, and they have forgotten what they have set out to do.

Our lives are like waves, and we have our up and down moments, with some areas more consistent than others. What do we do in those times where we make negative excuses?

We stop and refocus on the way we are living. We are in control, and the will-power we have is far greater than our circumstances.

The mind starts to race, and the body feels unbalanced, and tiredness sets in, then boom, we quit. We quit not because we are not strong enough, but because we did not know how far or how close we were.

Wow, I remember I never cried much when I felt hurt during my childhood, but it was the one moment in my life where I felt my body tighten, my spirit tired, my mind thinking hard, and I shut down.

That shut down was so life-changing for me that I told myself I will never come to that point ever again.

I stand here today to tell you do not let what you don't see affect what you see.

Your life's deepest thoughts are closer than you can imagine.

Do not give up.

This is your Breakdown; however, you will be built back up if you take action steps while riding the wave.

— — — — — ✍

CHAPTER 2

Peace & Soul

I have told many stories through my poetry, which I call 'StoryBook Poems', by which a Breakdown happened or was bound to happen if situations did not improve.

We have all been to The Breakdown, and many of us remain in that state because we have not recognized our souls.

Our souls need attention. The soul of human beings needs personal attention, and it cannot be suppressed or manipulated with money, drugs, alcohol, and/or other momentary items.

A practical method to bringing attention to your soul is beginning to sit quietly for 15 minutes at a time each day with a pen and paper, and write down what comes to your mind.

Do not use the excuse of how many hours you work or how full your schedule is. The 15 minutes is very manageable for everyone, think about how much time you spend each day on less important tasks, you can give 15 minutes to develop your life.

There is no timetable for how long you do the 15 minutes because every day is an opportunity for self-improvement.

Get comfortable with yourself, and most of all, get an understanding (Proverbs 4:7 KJV).

You will be surprised how much you will learn about yourself.

We are forever changing, and if we do not spend personal time with ourselves, we will always be closer to The Breakdown than we need to be.

– – – – – ✍

After you have spent 15 minutes at a time each day, I recommend fasting each month.

I understand that term is always seen through the lens of religious efforts. However, the term refers to cleansing the mind, body, and soul from all unrighteousness to realign our lives back to where they should be.

I recommend starting a week at a time. There are several fasts: meat, veggies, water, bread and water, etc.

- \ -

There is not one fast that is better than the other; it comes down to preference.

During your fast, you must take life easy. No working out, no hard labor, no drinking or smoking.

Just remember you are cleansing your body. Feel free to search the internet to find out information about fasting.

- \ -

The body is our temple, and we have to treat it as such. While researching which fast is best for you, I recommend not having too much information that you end up doing nothing, but just enough that you understand.

Remember, It is not a mistake that your Breakdown happens.

— — — — – ✍

Now, I have to take you through a process of recognition and steps to overcome The Breakdown. That's coming up in the next chapter...

Our lives are serious business, and it is important to pay attention to details. We make too many negative excuses with our lives, and as a result, we have invited chaos and confusion into our mind, body and souls.

I see too many people wondering why circumstances are happening in their lives over and over.

We can guess what happens next, they give up on themselves and go into a zero state, victim-minded, closed-channeled mindset.

-\-

I must remind you at this point that this message is not meant to condemn or convict anyone; however, you need to be set free from the cycle of The Breakdown and walk into glory. Your Destiny is important and needs to be manifested.

-\-

I believe the best-written books speak the truth, without worrying about whom it offends because the truth does not need to be validated by anyone's ignorance.

The truth remains the same no matter how much it is covered. The Breakdown is a serious matter and needs to be addressed delicately and intimately. It is yours to conquer with the right tools and mindset.

The Breakdown separates the employer from the employee, the truth from the lie, the wealthy from the rich, the 'haves' from the 'have nots'.

My goal is to bring you into the truth about yourself that you would stop and think and understand The Breakdown.

I always appreciated when I was told how great I am and all the glory words.

Nevertheless, I would have appreciated it more if I was provided an understanding of my emotions.

I learned on the run literally because I was a fast-paced individual. When I saw whatever I was looking for, I ran after it until I retrieved it.

_ _ _ _ _ ✍

Look around into our communities and on the television, we see so many people we perceive to be doing so well and having the glory road, but they still fail to maintain the proper stability.

Why?

The process of The Breakdown happened without them taking notice or not understanding what the process looks like.

You, my friends, are now aware.

The incomparable Maya Angelou says: "Do the best you can until you know better. Then when you know better, do better."

Now you know better!

CHAPTER 3

The Breakthrough

Now you have a practical and tangible idea about The Breakdown and how to improve yourself while going through its cycle.

This question is important, what is your next move?

You have to decide promptly and make it your duty to experience life in the fullest measure possible.

There is no benefit to not fulfilling your destiny. I read a post through social media saying, "A lot of people have million dollar ideas but a minimum wage work ethic."

Acknowledge your Breakdown because the outcome shall be beneficial. It takes work, and work like your life depends on it because it does.

Your legacy depends on it.

I speak with an urgent message because your lives affect each other.

For example, we see laws that are in place that many of us will look to and say that doesn't apply to me.

However, we must understand some laws are in place because of other individuals, but it covers the masses.

Take that with the same light of our parallel lifestyles. We can change our communities for the better or the worst by one choice or the lack of making a choice.

Get clear in your head as to what you want to accomplish.

––––––– ✍

The Breakdown must not be overlooked, and if you aren't careful, you will easily be discouraged by its cycle.

We must understand since we may no longer have the issues of old, it does not mean we are exempt from them attempting to return.

If we aren't careful and think of ourselves higher than we should, we will slip back into our old position.

So choose Today how you will handle The Breakdown: "the calm before the storm."

- ◈ Direct (Fight)
- ◈ Indirect (Flight/Freeze)

The Breakthrough Broken Down

On the other hand, there is an additional cycle needing to be uncovered, The Breakthrough.

Many of us have felt the emotional sense of The Breakthrough without the full understanding as to what had transpired.

Life is a series of attempts to accomplish specific projects. So as you are going about your life, remember you have a Breakthrough closer than your feelings or circumstances will sometimes allow you to see.

I am a convinced believer that our parents didn't talk to us with hateful messages or plant unrighteous seeds into our minds at birth when we were all born.

I am convinced they talked to us with loving, kind, and gentle words that we reacted to with a smile, or we listened as we laid quietly in the arms of our parents.

Please take notice of that process from the beginning because that started the process of our Breakthrough. The Breakthrough is "an instance of achieving success in a particular sphere, activity or obstacle."

The Breakthrough can and sometimes will be confused with The Breakdown.

The emotions are similar to two of the four emotions: fear and loss; additional emotions, including joy and confidence, are powerful and sometimes overlooked emotions during The Breakthrough process.

We have been conditioned to understand more of our negative emotions than our positive or what I like to call our growth emotions.

Each of our emotions can assist us with our growth if they are properly attended to. We cannot have The Breakthrough without The Breakdown.

Each one feeds off the other and works to improve our individual character.

CHAPTER 4

Breakthrough Your Mind

The Breakthrough shall be noticed when there is a connection with where you are and where you need to go.

In the realm of life, it is important to understand how life transitions from good to bad and bad to good.

An example is a change in close relationships. We must pay attention to how our friendships change because as our identity is formed, we begin to gain friends who go along with that lifestyle.

The saying is 'you are whom you hang around'.

That is true for several reasons. If a person wants to change his party habits, would it be wise to spend the majority of his or her time with people who party all the time?

If a person wants to stop drinking or quit smoking, should he spend most of his or her time with those individuals?

Those examples are pushing limits; however, my point is made about understanding whom you spend time with and how it will affect your living habits.

I know some believe they can live a lifestyle they don't personally accept. However, that is a conflict of interest, and it is important not to manipulate the mind.

Remember, the mind is powerful and easy to be easily manipulated.

The Process

The Breakthrough happens whether we are ready or not. It is important to stay prepared because opportunities change like the seasons, and if you have to say 'No', you need to make sure it is clear and if you have to say 'Yes', make sure it is clear.

- \ -

Don't second guess yourself because you haven't prepared yourself for the possible answers.

First, The Breakthrough starts as a:

- Thought(S)
- A Dream and/or Several Days of That Dream
- Goal(S) and/or Objective(S)

That unction that we feel in our spirit, some people call it the "gut feeling," is part of The Breakthrough process.

The unction is the sense of knowing something is changing. I mentioned earlier about our friendships/relationships; we must stay clear within our minds and away from toxic situations as much as possible.

Our Breakthrough can and will be missed if we choose to lose focus. If you do not program yourself, life will program you.

- \ -

The Breakthrough as 'thought' creates the atmosphere for action steps. The action steps are broad in scope to begin with; however, once we slow down and begin to think about what is happening, there is the opportunity for constructive and positive change to happen.

The examples of the thoughts and action steps are, but not limited to:

- ◆ Lack of desire of antisocial behaviors (ex. arguing, fighting, spend time in areas of toxic energy)

- The revisiting of those same ideas you once let go (beginning to change thinking patterns)

- You see/hear your ideas on tv, within conversations, or right in front of you

- The conversations you have started to become different (purposeful conversations)

Your body starts to feel different, and your spirit has the feeling of either tiredness or/ waking up. This is so important... we are sensitive because it is easy to mistake the breakdown and your breakthrough within this area.

— — — — – ✍

Relationships start to evolve–peer groups and other intimate relationships.

These are critical steps because many people can get lost and walk in the wilderness of their life and waste precious time, and I know you do not want to waste any more time.

-\-

**I am a living testimony of a life lived that took too long to get planted into its purpose. **

-\-

We cannot excuse ourselves or feel like it is okay to step off course. Our life depends on capitalizing on our breakthroughs because it keeps us consistent with the world's operations.

Remember this one truth: our life is just as important as the lesser or the greater person.

Our daily behaviors will allow us to walk, or not walk, in our purpose.

I love the saying: We could be doing the right thing at the wrong time and not get the right results (Unknown Source).

These action steps are critical to walk out and understand because a lot of us are further along with our Breakthrough than we understand.

————🖎

After the beginning has been established and identified that The Breakthrough is happening, plant the seeds into the areas that align with your goals/objectives.

My focus is youth and community; therefore, I have established 'StoryBook Poems' to target those areas.

When we begin the process of our Breakthrough, it may feel like a rush. Just like the wind blew open the door, and now every possible blessing and or the trials are happening.

That is why the beginning action steps are so important to take hold of, because we will have to say 'No' to some if not many opportunities.

You will have to be very clear in your mind and prepared to move according to what you want to decide.

This is the step where many people fail, and they fail because:

- ❖ Unfocused
- ❖ Lack of seriousness

- ◈ Misunderstanding
- ◈ Fear
- ◈ Unnecessary repetition
- ◈ Overthinking
- ◈ Not wanting to let go (change habits or create better habits)

For example, a person may not have let go of the friendships they should have let go of, or allowed their negative emotions to carry them.

I believe these are the two most important reasons for falling short in our Breakthrough.

Sometimes it does more damage to hold on than to let go. I am not saying a person should give up their relationships just because, but what I am saying is recognizing whether those that surround you are assets or liabilities.

Do not allow your life to be held back for the sake of friendships or short-term feelings. You have a destiny to reach in your life, and it important for you to live in that purpose.

As I mentioned earlier, there is no benefit to not walking according to your plan and purpose for your life.

Do you want to have regrets?

— — — — — ✍

The steps will assist us to identify with people in the positions we need. The idea of being "self-made" is irresponsible and senseless because none of us would exist or have any type of success without another person or person(s).

Each part of The Breakthrough is important, and each one makes the next one stronger.

I love this part because as I am teaching my youth daily, I point out this key... other people have been involved with their Breakthrough whether they ask them to be or not.

- \ -

The example I use is going to the doctor for an emergency procedure. I tell them to imagine if that person would not have lived out their life's purpose, then that procedure would not have gotten accomplished at that very moment when they needed it, and it is not always as simple as going to the "next" person.

So align your life with your purpose because you have what it takes, and the time is now.

-\-

You said tomorrow yesterday, and today is that tomorrow, so act now!

-\-

There are no same Breakthrough outcomes, but there are similarities that stand: they will happen, they are timely, specific to you, and can be missed.

There is not a set position by which any person receives their Breakthrough. If you want your Breakthrough, then position yourself accordingly, as I have mentioned.

I do not want you to be out of place and never receive the positions you should because you will always feel something is "missing" in your life.

We already have too many complacent people in the world, so do not add to the number. Instead, put yourself in the category of having a fulfilling life.

I want to make it very clear: Nothing will be given to you. If you are out of position, then you will miss out.

We see it all the time; people repeatedly ask for opportunities while they have not done their part to position themselves.

This type of thinking is insane—doing the same thing over and over while expecting different results.

CHAPTER 5

Types of Breakthrough

The Breakthrough is what we all want even if we are not willing to put in the work, but we want it to happen.

Take a look at social media or around in our society. We see many people who talk about the "grind or hustle."

The outcome we want is to have an improved life or, in other words, The Breakthrough.

-\-

I do not want to minimize the effort needed to reach and walk in your Breakthrough.

We need to add Delayed Gratification and Focus to the ingredients because much of what we will do will depend on how well we manage our time, how patient we are, how much focus we develop, and our commitment level to our life's purpose.

This is what a business Breakthrough looks like:

- ◈ The idea
- ◈ The steps of applying the idea develop in our mind's strategy, dotting the "i" and crossing to "t"

- Connections with specific people are building to establish the outcome

- Our friendships shifting and growing

- Delayed gratification and focus are being instituted

- The outcome is accessed

That is an example of the process for your Breakthrough.

The word 'business' should not hinder you from thinking it does not apply to you because you are not a business owner or entrepreneur.

I used the term 'business' because I know many people want a business breakthrough as well as a relationship Breakthrough.

–––––✍

The relationship Breakthrough is similar: (but not limited to)

- ◆ The unsettling thought (i.e. irritation, mentally tired, non-complacent thoughts)

- ◆ Changing of interaction styles (i.e.. more intimate or less intimate, sometimes fewer words towards each other or more open conversations, a new excitement with each other)

- ◆ Environment changes (i.e. job promotions, wage raises, opportunity to travel more)

- ◆ Milestones (i.e. both sides are seeing goals accomplished, short and long term goals, support from one another)

When it happens more than once, that is some of the best times and some of the most intensive times in our life.

Joy comes out of it, and character is being built. This is where your focus needs to be high and precise because you will have to say 'No' to a lot of distractions during this point.

When you are bomb rushed with friends' issues, work issues, car issues, family issues, etc., it will seem overwhelming; but hold on and slow down.

Here are some examples of how to remain focused and precise: (but not limited to)

▷ Quiet your life 15-30 minutes daily (have a pen and/or paper, not phone) write out your thoughts/goals.

▷ Prayer and fast (clean up your eating habits and social habits) set a daily time to pray and research different types of fasts. I encourage you to begin a weekend or a week at a time for fasting. This is not about any religion, but more importantly, aligning your mind, body, and soul.

▷ Be consistent daily - set the daily goal, and at the end of the day, make a list of 5 things you did not accomplish in the current day. Those items will carry over into the next day.

▷ Set mid weekly and weekly goals (Wednesday and Friday) and be specific. Do not overthink; make the goals practical and make them around your schedule.

— — — — — ✍

Self-management is important. However, commitment is needed to see the changes you want.

Commit to your life with a heavy sense of urgency. With that being said, your Breakthrough has been introduced, so now take hold of your life.

The lives we live are not supposed to be complicated; they are supposed to make sense in practical formation. We have heard the saying "life is hard."

I'd like to challenge that statement because once you understand life as a series of attempts to accomplish specific projects, then you know you have no other reason than to find out what you have to do to live out your Destiny.

If you can see it in your mind and you have the courage to speak it and commit to doing the daily work, it shall come to pass.

During this process of the Breakthrough, you do not have to know how it will happen; you have to be prepared to receive and be committed to doing your part, action steps.

- \ -

Take a moment right now and look over your life; everything you have up to this point happened because of the person you are.

- \ -

If you are not satisfied with the outcome, change who you are and watch your life change.

When I realized, "I am the master of my fate, I am the captain of my soul," life opened up to me and provided me with the necessary additions for me to live in my Destiny.

— — — — — ✍

Who are you today? You have to become obsessed with finding out your power place.

There is no benefit for you <u>not</u> to walk according to your plan and purpose. Take personal responsibility to position yourself.

Say to yourself:

- It is necessary for me to reach my destiny

- I do not have to prove myself to anyone

- My words are not just words; they are the doorway into my destiny

- It won't be easy, but I have the ability to accomplish all that I set in motion

- My friendships will change

- I am the environment I set up for myself

- How I live today will affect my children's children

- I am committed to doing my daily work

––––– ✍

Those affirmations are the stepping stones for your life as you put the work in, but you must follow those affirmations with action steps.

Impossible is just a big word for the time being when you don't have the proper vision.

The greatest gifts to the world were created by people who questioned the impossible: Dr. Martin Luther King Jr., Shirley Chisholm, Doug Williams, Marcus Garvey, Fredrick Douglas, Garrett Morgan, Maya Angelou, and Viola Davis, to name a few.

Each one of them did the "impossible." I challenge everyone not to find negative excuses, but to make results.

It is natural to have an automated sense of changing when we are uncomfortable. I challenge you to change into the person you want to become for the long haul.

If you settle today because you're tired or you don't know "what to do," you will have a void in your life.

$$- - - - - \text{✍}$$

As I started walking into my plan and purpose, it created more distractions. However, more importantly, people started to enter like never before.

My relationships changed, I had a different appetite for social activities because I was going into a higher atmosphere.

$$- \backslash -$$

Our Breakthroughs should elevate us into a higher atmosphere.

I would rather climb a hill with items useful for my improvement than items that weigh down my mind, body, and soul. This is a common reality for us.

Connect to Dots

The Breakdown and The Breakthrough need to be understood.

We shift from both so much that we need to handle both with a clear conscience that is not backed with negative emotions.

Let us face it, emotions are inconsistent and can easily be affected if we are not eating correctly and/or spending time with toxic media and/or friends.

This is a relevant book to add to your collection of personal development and personal empowerment.

After reading Seasonal Shifts, you are more equipped to stabilize your life and manage the process.

I know you will agree that when going into a new territory of your life, you better appreciate if you can know what is happening through the entire growth and development process rather than having to guess.

I want to encourage you to study the material within this book with a sharp eye and open your spirit.

- \ -

❀ It is HARD, easy living is not possible, but you can live comfortably and in peace.

- It is HARD when you have a family and a career;

- It is HARD when you invest your time and energy into something, and it fails

- It is HARD when you are living comfortably with your family, and your parents or other relatives pass away

- It is HARD when you have been working on the job for 20 plus years, and you get laid off

- It is HARD when you keep trying and trying, and you come up short

- It is HARD.

The situations we will face within our lives are heavy and tiring. You may even tell yourself that you are no good.

You may have used drugs to comfort your pain. You have said over and over, "I'm in hell."

Well, today is a great day for you because you have been provided the opportunity to add more understanding to your life.

It is time to change your thinking. It is time to change some friends. It is time to change your life!

– – – – – ✍

Here is something to live by, "you know better so you do better and now you who is reading this knows better."

Do not take anything for granted because one life is all we have been blessed to be in these physical bodies. It is important to know your life has a strong meaning, and my purpose will always be to assist you with being whom you are called to be.

This message is a turning point in your life. I know many people have always asked the question of why what, and how?

It is important to have the necessary equipment while you live. It is not easy to live when instability is around us.

What is written within this book is already within you. Start to be honest with yourself and come to the point in your life where you will no longer settle for the negative excuses.

What your life is, is who you are.

- \ -

The Breakdown and The Breakthrough are areas of our lives that are unavoidable.

We need balance.

Balance is our common goal. You no longer have to look for answers about what you're going through because now you have practical awareness and tools.

It is time to apply and live a changed lifestyle.

Be well and remain Blessed!

ABOUT THE AUTHOR

Amas Israel

StoryBook Poet

Amas Israel, aka The StoryBook Poet, is a Master Spoken Word Artist, Published Author, Youth Empowerment Champion and an Exuberant Orator who has improved the living conditions of hundreds of families and youth with mentorship in parenting, connecting community resources and promoting healthy relationships.

He launched a dynamic Youth Empowerment platform that instructs poetry and business modeling concepts to promote self-awareness and entrepreneurship.

StoryBook Enterprises LLC consists of Poetry, Publishing and Radio. Amas has written 5 Op-Ed articles for the Telegraph Herald newspaper surrounding the topic: Community Relationships, Youth Empowerment and Community Activism.

Follow Amas Israel on Social Media:

- ‣ Facebook: @storybookpoet
- ‣ Instagram: @storybookpoet
- ‣ Twitter: @storybookpoet

www.ingramcontent.com/pod-product-compliance
Lightning Source LLC
Chambersburg PA
CBHW052156090426
42741CB00010B/2292